to Katie

Happy Valentine's Day!

We ♡ you,

— Dad and Suz

Feb, 2007

TIMELESS THOUGHTS
ON *Love*

TIMELESS THOUGHTS
ON *Love*

An Anthology of Quotations

The Five Mile Press

The Five Mile Press Pty Ltd
70 Gold Street
San Francisco, CA 91433
USA
Website: www.fivemile.com.au
Email: publishing@fivemile.com.au

First published 2006
Compiled by Maggie Pinkney
Designed by Zoë Murphy
Illustration by Kieran Murphy
Printed in China
ISBN 1 74178 261 9

CONTENTS

PREFACE

The euphoria of being in love is universal, and has been experienced by succeeding generations down the centuries. No other theme has inspired so many profound poems and expressions of idealism.

In this intensely romantic anthology some of the finest writers the world has produced, from ancient to modern times, share their reflections on the subject of love; its joys and disappointments; its translucent beauty; its ability to evoke the best in all of us.

Also included is a selection of florid Victorian Valentine verse which reveals the extravagant passions that simmered beneath the surface of that purportedly strait-laced era. Although the expression of sincere emotions, most of these rhymes are over-sentimental to modern sensibilities. And yet they poignantly evoke a vanished era.

With its combination of charm and emotional wisdom, this collection is dedicated to all who are – or ever have been – in love.

Maggie Pinkney, 2006

LOVE IS ...

Love is

the wisdom of the fool,

and the folly of the wise.

SAMUEL JOHNSON, 1709–1784
English lexicographer, critic and essayist

Love is

of all the passions the strongest,

for it attacks simultaneously

the head, the heart, and the senses.

VOLTAIRE, 1694–1778
French philosopher, historian and writer

Love is an act
of endless forgiveness,
a tender look
that becomes a habit.

PETER USTINOV, 1921–2004
Russian-born English actor, dramatist and writer

Love is

the only sane and satisfactory answer

to the problem of human existence.

———

ERICH FROMM, 1900–1980
American psychoanalyst

Love is,

above all,

the gift of oneself.

JEAN ANOUILH, 1910–1987
French dramatist

Love is patient and kind;

love is not jealous or boastful;

it is not arrogant or rude.

Love does not insist on its own way;

it is not easily angered;

it keeps no records of wrongs.

———————————

1 CORINTHIANS 13: 4–8

Love is

the poetry of the senses.

HONORÉ DE BALZAC, 1799–1850
French writer

Love is

but the discovery

of ourselves in others,

and the delight

in the recognition.

———————

ALEXANDER SMITH, 1830–1867
Scottish poet

Love is like quicksilver in the hand.

Leave the fingers open and it stays.

Clutch it and it darts away.

———————

DOROTHY PARKER, 1893–1967
American writer and satirist

Love is

a symbol of eternity.

It wipes out all sense of time,

destroying all memory of a beginning

and all fear of an end.

MADAME DE STAËL, 1766 –1817
French writer and critic

Love is

a fiend, a fire,
a heaven, a hell,
Where pleasure, pain and
sad repentance dwell.

RICHARD BARNFIELD, 1574–1627
English poet

Love is

the greatest refreshment in life.

PABLO PICASSO, 1881–1973
Spanish painter and sculptor

Love is when

the other person's happiness

is more important than your own.

H. JACKSON BROWN, JR.
American writer and anthologist

Love is

a canvas furnished
by Nature
and embroidered
by imagination.

VOLTAIRE, 1694–1778
French philosopher, historian and writer

Love is

composed of a single soul
inhabiting two bodies.

ARISTOTLE, 384–322 BC
Greek philosopher

Love is

always bestowed as a gift –

freely, willingly, and without expectation.

We don't love to be loved;

we love to love.

LEO BUSCAGLIA, 1924–1998
American academic and writer

Love is

the expansion of two natures

in such a fashion

that each includes the other,

each is enriched by the other.

———————

FELIX ADLER, 1851–1933
German-born American intellectual and rationalist

Love is all we have,

the only way that each

can help the other.

EURIPIDES, c. 485–406 BC
Greek dramatist and poet

Love is

an irresistible desire
to be irresistibly desired.

ROBERT FROST, 1874–1963
American poet

Love is

everything it's cracked up to be …

It really is worth fighting for,

being brave for,

risking everything for.

———————

ERICA JONG, b. 1942
American writer and poet

Love is my religion.

JOHN KEATS, 1795–1821
English poet

IN LOVE

I ne'er was struck before that hour

With love so sudden and so sweet;

Her face it bloomed like a sweet flower

And stole my heart away complete.

JOHN CLARE, 1793–1864
English poet

But to see her

was to love her,

love but her,

and love forever.

ROBERT BURNS, 1759–1796
Scottish poet

I do not think that what is called Love at first sight is so great an absurdity as it is sometimes imagined to be. We generally make up our minds beforehand to the sort of person we should like, grave or gay, brown or fair; with golden tresses or raven locks; and when we meet with a complete example of the qualities we admire, the bargain is soon struck.

WILLIAM HAZLITT, 1778–1820
English essayist

We love being in love;

that's the truth on't.

WILLIAM MAKEPEACE THACKERAY, 1811–1863
English novelist

When love is not madness

it is not love.

PEDRO CALDERON DE LE BARCA, 1600–1681
Spanish dramatist

Jenny kiss'd me when we met,

    Jumping from the chair she sat in;

Time, you thief, who love to get

    Sweets into your list, put that in!

Say I'm weary, say I'm sad,

    Say that health and wealth have miss'd me,

Say I'm growing old, but add,

    Jenny kiss'd me.

LEIGH HUNT, 1784–1859
English poet, essayist and editor

This sensation of

listlessness, weariness, stupidity,

this disinclination to sit down

and employ myself,

this feeling of everything's being

dull and insipid about the house –

I must be in love.

JANE AUSTEN, 1775–1817
English novelist

It's curious how,

when you're in love,

you yearn to go about doing

acts of kindness to everybody.

———————

P.G. WODEHOUSE, 1881–1975
English humorous novelist

The moment you have in your heart

this extraordinary thing called love

and feel the depth, delight,

the ecstasy of it,

you will discover that for you

the world is transformed.

―――

JIDDU KRISHNAMURTI, 1895–1986
Indian-born spiritual leader

This was love at first sight,

love everlasting: a feeling unknown,

unhoped for, unexpected – in so far as

it could be a matter of conscious awareness;

it took entire possession of him,

and he understood with joyous amazement,

that this was for life.

THOMAS MANN, 1875–1955
German writer and critic

How did the party go in Portman Square?

I cannot tell you; Juliet wasn't there.

And how did Lady Gaster's part go?

Juliet was next me and I do not know.

HILAIRE BELLOC, 1870–1953
English essayist and writer of humorous verse

S trange how the heart will leap

To see one face at the door,

To hear one voice ring floating out,

One step upon the floor!

———————

MARY GILMORE, 1865–1962
Australian poet and journalist

I cannot fix the hour,

or the spot,

or the look,

or the words

which laid the foundation.

It is too long ago.

I was in the middle

before I knew I had begun.

JANE AUSTEN, 1775–1817
English novelist

He could not be mistaken.

There were no other eyes in the world like hers.

There was only one being in the world

who was able to concentrate for him

the whole world and the meaning of life.

It was she.

It was Kitty.

LEO TOLSTOY, 1828–1910
Russian novelist

Perhaps the feelings

that we experience when we are in love

represent a normal state.

Being in love shows a person

who he should be.

ANTON CHEKHOV, 1860–1904
Russian writer and dramatist

The meeting of

two personalities

is like the contact of

two chemical substances:

if there is any reaction,

both are transformed.

CARL JUNG, 1875–1961
Swiss psychiatrist

Doubt thou the stars are fire;

Doubt that the sun doth move;

Doubt truth to be a liar;

But never doubt I love.

———————

WILLIAM SHAKESPEARE, 1564–1616
English dramatist and poet

YOU, AND YOU ALONE

I wake filled with thoughts of you.

Your portrait and the intoxicating evening

which we spent together yesterday

have left my senses in turmoil.

Sweet, incomparable Josephine,

what a strange effect

you have on my heart!

NAPOLEON BONAPARTE, 1769–1821
French emperor

You, and you alone,

make me feel that I am alive.

Other men, it is said,

have seen angels,

but I have seen thee,

and thou art enough.

GEORGE MOORE, 1852–1933
Irish writer and dramatist

You have been mine before –

How long ago I may not know:

But just when at that swallow's soar

Your neck turned so,

Some veil did fall, – I knew it all of yore.

DANTE GABRIEL ROSSETTI, 1828–1882
English poet and painter

Your words are my food,
your breath my wine.
You are everything to me.

SARAH BERNHARDT, 1844–1923
French-born British actress

Come live with me and be my Love,

And we will all the pleasures prove

That hills and valley, dales and fields,

Or woods or steepy mountain yields.

CHRISTOPHER MARLOWE, 1564–1593
English poet and dramatist

I cannot exist without you.

I am forgetful of everything

but seeing you again –

my Life seems to stop there –

I see no further.

———————

JOHN KEATS, 1795–1821
English poet

What irresistible impulse

drove me toward you?

For an instant I saw the abyss.

I realised its depth

and then vertigo swept over me.

GUSTAVE FLAUBERT, 1821–1880
French writer

What I do and what I dream

include thee,

as the wine must taste

of its own grapes.

———

ELIZABETH BARRETT BROWNING, 1806–1861
English poet

O speak again, bright angel! – for thou art

As glorious to this night, being o'er my head,

As is a winged messenger of heaven

Unto the white-upturned wondering eyes

Of mortals that fall back to gaze upon him

When he bestrides the lazy, puffing clouds

And sails upon the bosom of the air.

WILLIAM SHAKESPEARE, 1564–1616
English dramatist and poet

I think of love, and you,

and my heart grows full and warm,

and my breath stands still …

I can feel a sunshine stealing into my soul

and making it all summer,

and every thorn,

a rose.

———————————

EMILY DICKINSON, 1830–1886
American poet

I have spread my dreams

under your feet.

Tread softly because

you tread on my dreams.

W.B. YEATS, 1865–1939
Irish poet and writer

I shall love you
until death do us part,
and then we shall be together
for ever and ever.

———————————

DYLAN THOMAS, 1914–1953
Welsh poet

Drink to me only with thine eyes,

And I will pledge with mine;

Or leave a kiss but in the cup

And I'll not look for wine.

BEN JONSON, 1572–1637
English dramatist and poet

You're more than an image
I dream about and cherish –
you are my superstition.

CHARLES BAUDELAIRE, 1821–1867
French poet

When you look at me, when you think of me, I am in Paradise.

WILLIAM MAKEPEACE THACKERAY, 1811–1863
English novelist

My life
has been awaiting you,
Your footfall was
my own heart's beat.

CONSTANTINE CAVAFY, 1863–1933
Greek poet

How do I love thee?

Let me count the ways.

I love thee to the depth

and breadth and height

My soul can reach …

I love thee with the breath,

Smiles, tears of all my life! –

and if God choose,

I shall but love thee better after death.

ELIZABETH BARRETT BROWNING, 1806–1861
English poet

UNREQUITED LOVE

Pains of love be sweeter far

Than all the other pleasures are.

JOHN DRYDEN, 1631–1700
English poet, satirist and dramatist

The love that lasts longest is the love that is never returned.

SOMERSET MAUGHAM, 1874–1965
English writer and dramatist

Let no one who loves

be called altogether unhappy.

Even love unreturned

has its rainbow.

J. M. BARRIE, 1860–1937
Scottish dramatist and writer

You never lose
by loving.
You always lose
by holding back.

BARBARA DEANGELIS, b. 1951
American talk show hostess

Nothing takes

the taste out of peanut butter

like unrequited love.

CHARLES M. SCHULZ, 1922–2000
American cartoonist

You'll put on weight, take it off,

cry at advertisements for bathroom accessories,

drink too much, let pot-plants die,

shout at relatives … and forget to pay the rent.

But remember that people who have never had a

broken heart will never understand dead roses,

Tolstoy, airport lounges, Albinoni's Adagio in G minor,

neat brandy, the moon, and drizzle.

WENDY HARMER, b. 1951
Australian journalist and comedian

Why doesn't one just die automatically when left by the person one loves?

VIOLET KEPPEL, 1894–1970
Daughter of King Edward VII's mistress, Alice Keppel

It is best to love wisely, no doubt.

But to love foolishly

is better than not to be able

to love at all.

———————

WILLIAM MAKEPEACE THACKERAY, 1811–1863
English novelist

Oh, life is a glorious cycle of song

A medley of extemporanea;

And love is a thing that can never go wrong;

And I am Marie of Romania

DOROTHY PARKER, 1893–1967
American writer and satirist

To fear love is to fear life;
and those who fear life
are already three parts dead.

BERTRAND RUSSELL, 1872–1970
British philosopher, mathematician and writer

Alas, my love! you do me wrong

To cast me off discourteously,

For I have loved you so long,

Delighting in your company.

Greensleeves was all my joy,

Greensleeves was my delight.

Greensleeves was my heart of gold.

Yea, who but my lady Greensleeves.

16TH-CENTURY SONG

Give me a dozen such heartbreaks

if that would help me

lose a couple of pounds.

COLETTE, 1873–1954
French writer

'Tis better to have loved and lost

Than never to have loved at all.

ALFRED, LORD TENNYSON, 1809–1892
English poet

Perhaps a great love
is never returned.

DAG HAMMARSKJÖLD, 1905–1961
Swedish statesman, Secretary-General of the United Nations

What the heart

has once owned and had,

it shall never lose.

All love is sweet,

given or returned.

Common as light is love,

and its familiar voice

wearies not ever.

―――――――――

PERCY BYSSHE SHELLEY, 1792–1822
English poet

To love and win

is the best thing.

To love and lose,

the next best.

WILLIAM MAKEPEACE THACKERAY, 1811–1863
English novelist

REFLECTIONS ON LOVE

Love looks not with the eyes,

but with the mind,

And therefore

is winged Cupid blind.

WILLIAM SHAKESPEARE, 1564–1616
English dramatist and poet

Love does not consist

of gazing at each other,

but in looking together

in the same direction.

———————

ANTOINE DE SAINT-EXUPÉRY, 1900–1944
French writer and aviator

Love, as is told by the seers of old,

Comes as a butterfly tipped with gold,

Flutters and flies in sunlit skies,

Weaving 'round hearts that were one time cold.

ALGERNON SWINBURNE, 1837–1909
English poet

The madness of love
is the greatest
of heaven's blessings.

PLATO, c. 429–347 BC
Greek philosopher

The most powerful symptom of love

is a tenderness which becomes

almost insupportable.

VICTOR HUGO, 1802–1885
French poet, writer and dramatist

What is love?: 'tis not hereafter;

Present mirth hath present laughter;

What's to come is still unsure;

In delay there lies no plenty;

Then come kiss me, sweet and twenty,

Youth's a stuff will not endure.

WILLIAM SHAKESPEARE, 1564–1616
English dramatist and poet

Love,

another religion,

has a style of its own.

The words of its fanatics are strange,

obscure, incoherent, and often

incomprehensible to all the world

save the initiated.

J.T. MERYDREW
English writer

All, everything that I understand,

I understand only because of love.

LEO TOLSTOY, 1828–1881
Russian novelist

The magic of the first love
is our ignorance
that it can ever end.

BENJAMIN DISRAELI, 1804–1881
English statesman and writer

Love does not begin and end

the way we seem to think it does.

Love is a battle, love is a war;

love is a growing up.

JAMES BALDWIN, 1924–1987
American writer

True love is but a humble, low-born thing,

   And hath its food served up in earthenware;

It is a thing to walk with, hand in hand,

   Through the everydayness of this workday world.

JAMES RUSSELL LOWELL, 1819–1891
American poet, abolitionist and diplomat

All love

that has not friendship for its base

is like a mansion

built upon the sand.

ELLA WHEELER WILCOX, 1850–1919
American writer

To love and be loved
is to feel the sun
from both sides.

DAVID VISCOTT, 1938–1996
American psychiatrist and author

What love we've given,

we shall have forever.

What love we fail to give,

will be lost for all eternity.

―――――――

LEO BUSCAGLIA, 1924–1998
American academic and writer

The heart has reasons
that reason
does not understand.

JACQUES-BENIGNE BOSSUET
French writer

All love at first, like generous wine,

Ferments and frets until 'tis fine;

But when 'tis settled on the lee,

And from th'impurer matter free,

Becomes the richer still the older,

And proves the pleasanter the colder.

—————

SAMUEL BUTLER, 1835–1902
English writer

The arms of love
encompass you with your present,
your past and your future;
the arms of love
gather you together.

ANTOINE DE SAINT EXUPÉRY, 1900–1944
Poet and pilot

Love unlocks
doors and windows
that weren't even
there before.

—————

MIGNON MCLAUGHLIN, 1913–1983
American journalist and author

Love to faults is always blind,

Always is to joy inclined,

Lawless, winged, and unconfin'd

And breaks all chains from every mind.

———————

WILLIAM BLAKE, 1757–1827
English poet

This is the true meaning of love:

when we believe that we alone can love,

that no one could ever have

loved so much before us,

and that no one will ever

love in the same way after us.

JOHANN WOLFGANG VON GOETHE, 1749–1832
German poet, writer, dramatist and statesman

Keep love in your heart.

A life without it is like

a sunless garden when the flowers are dead.

The consciousness of loving and being loved

brings a warmth and richness to life

that nothing else can bring.

—

OSCAR WILDE, 1854–1900
Irish dramatist, novelist and wit

Only love

can be divided endlessly

and still not be diminished.

─────────

ANNE MORROW-LINDBERGH, 1906–2001
American aviator and writer

Love is friendship that has caught fire.

It is quiet understanding, sharing and forgiving.

It is loyalty through good times and bad times.

It settles for less than perfection

and makes allowances for human weaknesses.

Love is content with the present,

it hopes for the future,

and it does not brood over the past.

It's the day-in and day-out chronicles

of irritations, problems, compromise,

small disappointments, big victories

and working toward common goals.

If you have love in your life, it can make up

for a great many things that are missing.

If you don't have love in your life,

no matter what else there is,

it's not enough.

ANN LANDERS, 1918–2002
American newspaper advice columnist

Love grows by giving.
The love we give away
is the only love we keep.
The only way to retain love
is to give it away.

ELBERT HUBBARD, 1856–1915
American editor and writer

The story of love

is not important – what is important

is that one is capable of love.

It is perhaps the only glimpse

we are permitted of eternity.

HELEN HAYES, 1900–1993
American actress

Love seeketh not itself to please

Nor for itself hath any care

But for another gives its ease

And builds a Heaven in Hell's despair.

WILLIAM BLAKE, 1757–1827
English poet

Love consists in this,

that two solitudes

protect and touch

and greet each other.

RAINER MARIA RILKE, 1875–1926
Austrian poet

Love alone is capable

of uniting human beings in such a way

as to complete and fulfill them,

for it alone takes them and joins them

by what is deepest in themselves.

———————

PIERRE TEILHARD DE CHARDIN, 1881–1955
French Jesuit priest

One word frees us
of all the weight
and pain of life;
that word is love.

SOPHOCLES, 496–406 BC
Greek tragedian

Love's not Time's fool, though rosy lips and cheeks

Within his bending sickle's compass come;

Love alters not with his brief hours and weeks,

But bears it out even to the edge of doom.

If this be error and upon me proved,

I never writ, nor no man ever loved.

WILLIAM SHAKESPEARE, 1564–1616
English dramatist and poet

Being deeply loved by someone
gives you strength;
loving someone deeply
gives you courage.

LAO TZU, c. 600 BC
Chinese philosopher

Wherever the wings of love take me,

that is my flare path and my way.

———

DIANE CILENTO, b. 1933
Australian actress and writer

VICTORIAN
VALENTINES

Take this token of affection.

May its beauty move thy heart.

Chill me not with cold rejection,

Bid not all my hopes depart!

When the golden sun is sinking

And your heart from care is free

When e'er a thousand things you're thinking

Will you sometimes think of me?

Tho far away from thee I roam,

Forget thee I can never;

For all the joy this life affords

Is centered in thee ever.

For Laura

Less of friendship, more of love,

A single smile, my heart can move;

Undying love! Not echoed yet,

Remains within a pond'rous weight

And, without you, I'm all but dead.

Accept this message,

Dearest, I pray,

From one who loves you,

'Tis Valentine's Day.

I know a heart in lady-land

So innocent and bright;

I know a dear and dainty hand

So warm, and wee, and white,

And lightly to the winds I'd cast

All else the world doth hold,

If I could bind them close and fast

Within a hoop of gold.

An emblem of this happy life

Unknown to care, devoid of strife

Where Beauty's self reposes.

May it prove so, with you and I

If Wedlock's Sweets we chance to try

With love among the Roses.

Name the day

sweet Valentine,

When Church and Ring

will make you Mine.

Tho' small the pledge, yet may it be

Remembrance of my love to thee,

And may thy love delight my breast,

Possessing all of thee possest.

I'd have, my love, a happy home,

(just what a home should be)

A home of peace, a home of love,

as made by thee and me,

When true affection warms the breast,

and dreams like these depart,

It matters little what's our lot,

love's home is in the heart.

The stars may fall, the sun decay,

The earth's whole fabric waver,

But firm as heaven my love shall stay,

Unquenched, unceasing never.

WEDDING BELLS

Ring sweetest bells, in merry peals,

Ring for the love that the eye reveals,

Ring for the vows that make two one,

Ring for the best day under the sun.

TRADITIONAL ENGLISH RHYME

Grow old along with me!
The best is yet to be.

ROBERT BROWNING, 1812–1889
English poet

To have and hold

from this day forward

for better or worse,

for richer or poorer,

in sickness and in health,

to love and to cherish,

till death us do part.

BOOK OF COMMON PRAYER

The Bridal Bouquet

And let them also with them bring in hand

Another gay garland

For my fair love, of lilies and roses,

Bound true-love-wise with a blue silk ribbon.

EDMUND SPENCER, 1532–1599
English poet

Something old,

something new

Something borrowed,

something blue.

OLD ENGLISH TRADITION

Marriage is an Athenic

weaving together of families,

of two souls with their

individual fates and destinies,

of time and eternity – everyday life

married to the timeless

mysteries of the soul.

———————

THOMAS MOORE
American psychiatrist and writer

To The Bride

When thy foot is at the altar,

When the ring hath press'd thy hand,

When those thou lov'st, and those who love thee,

Smiling round thee stand,

O, may the verse that friendship weaves,

Like a spirit of the air

Be o'er thee at that moment,

For a blessing and a prayer.

UNKNOWN

Now join hands,
and with your hands
your hearts.

WILLIAM SHAKESPEARE, 1564–1616
English dramatist and poet

As Roses other flowers excel

So Wedlock's charm still wears the bell

Among the joys of human life.

No pleasure can with these compare

Which faithful love alone can share

Twixt happy man and wife.

UNKNOWN

The Wedding Cake

Today, my Julia, thee must make,

For mistress bride an wedding cake;

Kneade but the dow, and it wille be,

Turned to prosperitie by thee.

Now the paste of almond fine

Assures a broode o' childer nine.

———

TRADITIONAL ELIZABETHAN RHYME

The Bride

The ring is on my hand,

And the wreath is on my brow,

Satins and jewels grand

Are all at my command,

And I am happy now.

EDGAR ALLAN POE, 1809–1849
American poet and writer

Let us celebrate
the occasion
with wine
and sweet words.

PLAUTUS, c. 254 – c. 184 BC
Roman playwright

The Wedding Ring

And as this round

Is nowhere found

To flaw, or else to sever,

So let our love

As endless prove

And pure as gold forever.

ROBERT HERRICK, 1592–1674
English poet

LOVE AND MARRIAGE

A good marriage has in it

all the pleasures of a friendship,

all the enjoyments of sense and reason,

and indeed all the sweets of life.

JOSEPH ADDISON, 1672–1719
English essayist and politician

Hail wedded love,

mysterious law,

true source

Of human happiness.

JOHN MILTON, 1608–1674
English poet

To My Wife

As far away alone I roam,

My thoughts are filled with love and home.

I listen in the sunset glow

For words and songs of long ago.

I think of all most dear to me

And with them all come

thoughts of thee.

UNKNOWN

Well, what is a relationship?

It's about two people having tremendous weaknesses and vulnerabilities, like we all do, and one person being able to strengthen the other in their areas of vulnerability. And vice versa. You need each other. You complete each other, passion and romance aside.

JANE FONDA, b. 1937
American actress and writer

A good marriage

is that in which

each appoints the other

guardian of his solitude.

RAINER MARIA RILKE, 1875–1926
Austrian poet

Marriage is that relation

between man and woman in which

the independence is equal,

the dependence mutual,

and the obligation reciprocal.

LOUIS K. ANSPACHER, 1878–1947
American dramatist

Marriage involves

big compromises all the time.

International-level compromises.

You're the USA, and he's the USSR

and you're talking nuclear warheads.

———————

BETTE MIDLER, b. 1945
American comedian, actor and singer

A successful marriage
is an edifice that
must be rebuilt
every day.

ANDRÉ MAUROIS, 1885–1967
French writer

Marriage is not a ritual or an end.

It is a long, intricate, intimate dance together,

and nothing matters more

than your own sense of balance,

and choice of partner.

———————

AMY BLOOM
American psychotherapist and novelist

Chains do not hold a marriage together.

It is threads, hundreds of tiny threads,

which sew people together through the years.

That is what makes a marriage last –

more than passion or even sex.

SIMONE SIGNORET, 1921–1985
French actress

Men and women

are made to love each other.

It's only by loving each other

they can achieve anything.

CHRISTINA STEAD, 1903–1983
Australian novelist

Partnership,

not dependence,

is the real romance

in marriage.

MURIEL FOX, b. 1928
American business executive

If ever two were one, then surely we,

If ever man were loved by wife, then thee;

If ever wife was happy in a man,

Compare with me, ye women, if you can.

I prize thy love more than whole mines of gold

Or all the riches that the East doth hold.

ANNE BRADSTREET, 1612–1672
English-born American poet

If you can find a truly good wife

she is worth more than precious gems!

When she speaks, her words are wise,

and kindness is the rule for everything.

———————

PROVERBS 31:10: 26
Old Testament

Married couples who love each other tell each other a thousand things without talking.

PORTUGUESE PROVERB

What greater thing is there

for two human souls

than to feel that they are joined …

to be at one with each other

in silent, unspeakable memories.

———————

GEORGE ELIOT, 1819–1880
English writer and poet

Give your hearts,

but not into each other's keeping.

For only the hand of Life can contain your hearts.

And stand together yet not too near together.

For the pillars of the temple stand apart,

And the oak tree and the cypress

grow not in each other's shadow.

———————

KAHLIL GIBRAN, 1883–1931
Lebanese poet, artist and mystic

A happy marriage

is a long conversation

that seems all too short.

ANDRÉ MAUROIS, 1885–1967
French dramatist and writer

An Old Wedding Ring

Your wedding ring wears thin, dear wife;

ah, summers not a few

Since I put it on your finger first

have passed o'er me and you;

And, love, what changes we have seen –

what cares and pleasures too –

Since you became my own dear wife,

when this old ring was new.

The past is dear, its sweetness still

our memories to reassure yet.

The griefs we've borne, together borne,

we would not now forget.

Whatever, wife, the future brings,

heart unto heart still true,

We'll share as we have shared all else

Since this old ring was new.

———————

UNKNOWN

A good marriage

is like Dr Who's Tardis,

small and banal from the outside,

but spacious and interesting

from within.

———————

KATHARINE WHITEHORN, b. 1928
English journalist and columnist

One should
believe in marriage
as in the immortality
of the soul.

HONORÉ DE BALZAC, 1799–1850
French novelist

Valentine to One's Wife

Hearts and darts and maids and men

Vows and valentines are here;

Will you give yourself again,

Love me for another year?

JOHN ERSKINE, 1879–1951
American educator, novelist and musician

A marriage

makes of two fractional lives a whole;

it gives to two purposeless lives a work,

and doubles the strength of each to perform it;

it gives to two questioning natures

a reason for living,

and something to live for.

MARK TWAIN, 1835–1910
American writer

The love we have in our youth

is superficial

compared to the love

an old man has for his wife.

WILL DURANT, 1885–1982
American philosopher and writer

Thee, Mary, with this ring I wed,

So, fourteen years ago, I said.

Behold another ring! For what?

With that first ring I married youth,

Grace, beauty, innocence and truth,

Taste long admired, sense long revered,

All my Molly then appeared,

If she by merit since disclosed,

Proved twice the woman I supposed,

I plead that double merit now,

To justify a double vow.

UNKNOWN

Love seems the swiftest,

but is the slowest of all growths.

No man or woman knows

what perfect love is

until they have been married

for a quarter of a century.

———

MARK TWAIN, 1835–1910
American writer

The ring so worn as you behold,

So thin, so pale, is yet of gold:

The passion such it was to prove;

Worn with life's cares, love yet was love.

―――――――――

GEORGE CRABBE, 1754–1832
English poet

She who dwells with me,

whom I have loved

With such communion,

that no place on earth

Can ever be a solitude to me.

_____

WILLIAM BLAKE, 1770–1850
English poet

WORDS OF WISDOM

It is by loving and not by being loved

that one can come nearest the soul of another;

yea where two love it is the loving of each other,

and not the being loved by each other,

that originates and perfects

and ensures their blessedness.

GEORGE MACDONALD, 1824–1905
Scottish writer and poet

What do we live for,

if it is not to make life

less difficult

for each other?

GEORGE ELIOT, 1819–1880
English writer and poet

The affirmation of one's own life,

happiness, growth, freedom

is rooted in one's capacity to love.

ERICH FROMM, 1900–1980
American psychoanalyst

Kindness in words
creates confidence.
Kindness in thinking
creates profoundness.
Kindness in giving
creates love.

LAO TZU, c. 600 BC
Chinese philosopher

There is no instinct
like that
of the heart.

LORD BYRON, 1788–1824
English poet

Once the realization is accepted

that even between the closest human beings

infinite distances continue,

a wonderful living side by side

can grow.

RAINER MARIA RILKE, 1875–1926
Austrian poet

Don't sacrifice your life
to work and ideals.

The most important things in life
are human relationships.

I found that out too late.

———————

KATHARINE SUSANNAH PRICHARD, 1883–1969
Australian writer

Let there be spaces
in your togetherness.

KAHLIL GIBRAN, 1883–1931
Lebanese poet, artist and mystic

Mercy is Love being gracious.

Faith is Love believing.

Charity is Love acting.

Sacrifice is Love offering itself.

Patience is Love waiting.

Endurance is Love abiding.

Hope is Love expecting.

Peace is Love resting.

Prayer is Love communing.

———————

UNKNOWN

To keep your marriage brimming

With love in the wedding cup,

Whenever you're wrong admit it;

Whenever you're right, shut up.

OGDEN NASH, 1902–1971
American humorous poet

For one human being to love another

is perhaps the most difficult of our tasks;

the ultimate, the last test and proof:

the work for which all other work

is but preparation.

———————

RAINER MARIA RILKE, 1875–1926
Austrian poet

A loving heart
is the
truest wisdom.

CHARLES DICKENS, 1812–1870
English novelist

Love one another, but make not

a bond of love;

Let it rather be a moving sea

between the shores of your souls.

Fill each other's cup, but drink not

from the one cup.

Give one another of your bread but eat

not from the same loaf.

Sing and dance together and be joyous,

but let each one of you be alone,

Even as the strings of a lute are alone though

they quiver with the same music.

KAHLIL GIBRAN, 1883–1931
Lebanese poet, artist and mystic

Find the person

who will love you

because of your differences,

and not in spite of them.

LEO BUSCAGLIA, 1924–1998
American academic and writer

Treasure the love

that you receive

above all.

It will survive long after

your gold and good health

have vanished.

───────────

OG MANDINO, 1923–1996
American author